Fossilized!
SEA CREATURE FOSSILS

By Kathleen Connors

Gareth Stevens
Publishing

Please visit our website, www.garethstevens.com. For a free color catalog of all our high-quality books, call toll free 1-800-542-2595 or fax 1-877-542-2596.

Library of Congress Cataloging-in-Publication Data

Connors, Kathleen.
Sea creature fossils / Kathleen Connors.
    p. cm. — (Fossilized!)
Includes index.
ISBN 978-1-4339-6430-5 (pbk.)
ISBN 978-1-4339-6431-2 (6-pack)
ISBN 978-1-4339-6428-2 (library binding)
1. Fishes, Fossil—Juvenile literature. I. Title.
QE851.C66 2012
567—dc23

                                        2011037101

First Edition

Published in 2013 by
Gareth Stevens Publishing
111 East 14th Street, Suite 349
New York, NY 10003

Designer: Katelyn E. Reynolds
Editor: Kristen Rajczak

Photo credits: Cover, pp. 1, 7, 12–13, 17, (cover, pp. 1, 3–24 background and graphics) Shutterstock.com; p. 5 David McNew/Getty Images; p. 6 Dorling Kindersley/Getty Images; p. 9 DEA/G. Cigolini/Getty Images; p. 11 Brandon Goldman/Flickr/Getty Images; p. 14 Colin Keates/Dorling Kindersley/Getty Images; p. 15 AFP/Getty Images; pp. 18–19 Valery Hache/AFP/Getty Images; p. 20 Xavier Rossi/Gamma-Rapho via Getty Images; p. 21 Hemera/Thinkstock.

Printed in the United States of America

CPSIA compliance information: Batch #CW12GS: For further information contact Gareth Stevens, New York, New York at 1-800-542-2595.

CONTENTS

Words in the glossary appear in **bold** type the first time they are used in the text.

UNDER THE SEA

From tiny **algae** to huge whales and fish, creatures big and small live in the sea. Some are linked to the oldest kinds of living things on Earth!

Plants and animals that lived thousands or millions of years ago left behind remains or marks. These are fossils. Scientists use fossils to learn more about how sea creatures changed over time to become those we know today. How did the fossils form? Read on to find out!

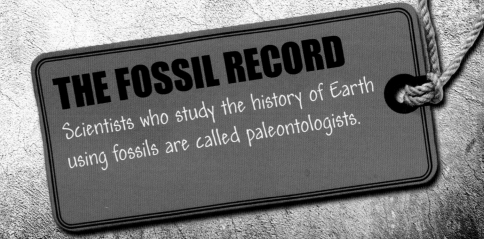

THE FOSSIL RECORD

Scientists who study the history of Earth using fossils are called paleontologists.

A paleontologist digs up whale fossils found in California. ▽

PRESERVED IN SEDIMENT

Marine, or ocean, **environments** offer good conditions for fossils to form—and not just for sea creatures. Many fossils are found near bodies of water because **sediment** is found on the bottom of oceans, rivers, and lakes.

In order for a fossil to form, an animal or plant first must be buried in sediment. Over time, great pressure turns the sediment into rock. This **preserves** the animal or plant matter. The soft parts often break down, leaving behind harder parts such as shells and bones.

This drawing shows a fish's bones that have been buried and preserved in a layer of rock.

THE FOSSIL RECORD

The soft parts of sea creatures are sometimes preserved, too. These fossils allow scientists to study what the creature looked like at the time it was buried in sediment.

Sea creature fossils have been found deep below the ocean's surface and in shallow waters like these in Thailand.

HOW SEA CREATURE FOSSILS FORM

The shells or hard **skeletons** of some ancient sea creatures are commonly found fossils. Shells and skeletons leave fossils because they don't break down easily. **Permineralization** (puhr-mih-nuh-ruhl-ih-ZAY-shun) fossilizes some of these parts.

Other sea creatures left a kind of fossil called a mold. A mold forms when a sea creature's whole body breaks down, leaving behind an open space inside the rock that bears the creature's shape.

Another type of fossil called a cast sometimes forms from a mold. This happens when **minerals** fill the mold.

THE FOSSIL RECORD

Sometimes, a sea creature leaves behind both a mold and a cast.

8

These fossils may be casts of ancient sea snails.

HOW OLD ARE THEY?

Some of the earliest **organisms** in the sea left behind fossils that are 3 billion years old! These fossils come from tiny creatures called cyanobacteria and have been found in Australia.

Fossils show more familiar sea creatures starting to appear about 542 million years ago, during a time period scientists call the Paleozoic era. Fish and jellyfish fossils date back about 500 million years. Scientists have learned from fossils that many marine **reptiles** first appeared between about 299 and 251 million years ago.

Cenozoic era	65.5 million years ago–present day
Mesozoic era	251–65.5 million years ago
Paleozoic era	542–251 million years ago
Precambrian era	4.6 billion–542 million years ago

This chart shows how scientists divide parts of Earth's history.

THE FOSSIL RECORD

The division of the long history of Earth is called the geologic time scale.

These are the fossils of an ancient sea animal called the sea lily.

EARLY SEA CREATURE FOSSILS

Two of the most common types of sea creature fossils come from trilobites and ammonites. Trilobite fossils may date back 542 million years! These ancient **arthropods** had an exoskeleton, or hard outer covering, that was shed as the trilobite grew. Because the exoskeletons didn't break down, many became fossilized.

Ammonite fossils are curved and pretty. They look a bit like seashells on a beach. They may be anywhere from about 416 to 65 million years old because many different kinds of ammonites lived in the sea over a long period of time.

Trilobite fossils like this one have been found all over the world.

THE FOSSIL RECORD

When the trilobites died out, other arthropods such as crabs and shrimp started to appear. Shrimp burrows, or the small tunnels shrimp made to live in, are common fossils.

PLESIOSAURS

Paleontologists have found fossils of larger sea creatures, too. Some of these were the **ancestors** of modern reptiles, such as turtles and snakes.

Plesiosaurs were one kind of marine reptile that left behind many fossils. They lived in the Pacific Ocean and the seas of what is now Europe. They swam using fins that looked like a sea lion's. Paleontologists have found fossils from two kinds of plesiosaurs: short-necked pliosaurs and the long-necked plesiosaurids. Their fossils date back about 215 to 80 million years.

This ancient plesiosaur's foot looks a bit like a human's!

THE FOSSIL RECORD

Pieces of fossilized plesiosaur skeletons have been uncovered near Japan, Australia, and New Zealand.

Fossils from a plesiosaur called *Kimmerosaurus* were found near Norway in 2004.

15

INDEX FOSSILS

Sea creature fossils have been helpful in making a timeline of life on Earth. Their fossils are often used as index fossils to figure out the age of other fossils.

Index fossils are chosen because they're easy to recognize and plentiful. They're a feature of a certain time period. For example, scientists know when different types of ammonites lived. If a fossil of one kind of ammonite is found in the same rock layer as the fossil of an ancient reptile, scientists can guess they lived at the same time.

THE FOSSIL RECORD

Trilobites are often used as index fossils.

Ammonite fossils like these were called "snakestones" before it was known they were fossilized sea creatures.

▽

17

RECENT FINDS

Paleontologists continue to uncover sea creature fossils that teach us what Earth was like long ago. In 2009, scientists found fossils of a huge pliosaur. Its head was two times the size of a *Tyrannosaurus rex*'s head!

In 2011, scientists in Alaska uncovered the most complete skeleton of a sea creature called a thalattosaur ever found in North America. Thalattosaurs, which looked like giant lizards, died out 200 million years ago.

THE FOSSIL RECORD

The pliosaur uncovered in 2009 was found on an Arctic island very close to the place where many other fossils of large marine reptiles have been found.

The fossils of this ancient marine reptile were found in Kansas. They're about 150 million years old.

FINDING FOSSILS

Paleontologists find sea creature fossils in some unlikely places. Sometimes, they find fossils on mountaintops! This is because the ground shifted after the sea creatures were buried and the sediment had turned to rock.

While sea creature fossils have been found in places as far apart as Morocco and Peru, the best way to see these fossils is at a museum. The Burke Museum of Natural History and Culture in Washington State has a large collection of sea creature fossils dating back about 80 million years.

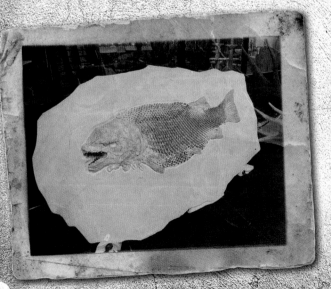

- Plesiosaurs were part of a group of ancient marine reptiles called sauropterygians (sohr-AHP-tuh-rih-gee-uhnz).

- Recent fossil finds show that modern whales come from animals that once lived on land. Millions of years ago, their bodies changed to suit a completely marine life.

- In 2011, scientists uncovered the biggest fossil ever found of a certain kind of marine turtle near Sewell, New Jersey. It was 3 feet (0.9 m) wide and about 65 million years old!

- Many trilobites were small. However, a trilobite fossil found near Boston, Massachusetts, shows one that was 18 inches (46 cm) long and may have weighed as much as 10 pounds (4.5 kg)!

GLOSSARY

algae: livings things that grow in water and make their own food, much like plants do

ancestor: an animal that lived before others in its family tree

arthropod: one of a group of animals with an exoskeleton and a body divided into parts

environment: surroundings

mineral: matter found in nature that is not living

organism: a living thing

permineralization: a process of fossilization in which a mixture of water and minerals flow into a dead organism and fill its empty spaces

preserve: to keep from breaking down completely

reptile: an animal covered with scales or plates that breathes air, has a backbone, and lays eggs, such as a turtle, snake, lizard, or crocodile

sediment: matter, like stone and sand, that is carried onto land or into the water by wind, water, or land movement

skeleton: the bony frame of the body

FOR MORE INFORMATION

Books

Arnold, Caroline. *Giant Sea Reptiles of the Dinosaur Age.*
New York, NY: Clarion Books, 2007.

Dixon, Dougal. *Prehistoric Oceans.* Mankato, MN:
NewForest Press, 2011.

Websites

Paleontology: The Big Dig
www.amnh.org/ology/paleontology
Learn more about fossils and what paleontologists do when
they find them.

Sea Monster Pictures
animals.nationalgeographic.com/animals/photos/sea-monster-gallery
Look at pictures and read about what sea creatures might
have been like millions of years ago.

INDEX